The Bear
Who Came
To Town

poems by John Koehler

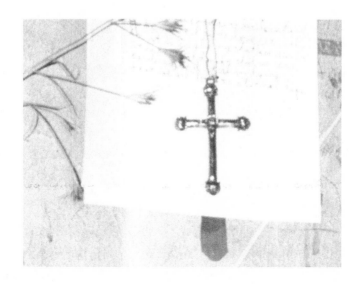

SPUYTEN DUYVIL
New York City

ISBN 978-1-956005-75-2

LCCN: 2022938568

The Bear Who Came To Town

Cuba Lake, N.Y. *From a standing position, looking inward...*

CONTENTS

INTRODUCTION

I always think of John as a poet. In my work, I have met and known many creative people who call themselves poets, and I have read a great many more; only some of them are the real thing. Most poets in the culture industry are made conspicuous, like the Straw Man for his diploma, by prizes, degrees, and readings. John never presumed to identify himself by the title of poet, and only reluctantly, you might even say humbly, at age 40, did he post a first selection of his poems online. But he wrote—he wrote poems on every surface in his room, not neglecting walls, furniture, the CD player, and the window sill, so that he lived inside his own collage, a naïve Schwitters in his Merzbau—and he carefully revised his work: this is what a poet does. And in his lines, John was whole, a bold believer who went with the ebbs and flows of language, forever falling in love anew with the world his God for some reason created. I hold an unprovable theory that innumerable Frosts and Dickinsons and write immortal poems that, for lots of reasons, never get read. John Koehler has long been among that honest company.

The poet was the eighth of nine children born to a high school English teacher and a future nurse. The two siblings nearest in age to John both made professors of English in other states. His parents came to Hornell as a young married couple from Rochester, New York, and became highly valued citizens in the life and work of the local school, hospital, and parish. John Francis Koehler was born on July 19, 1967, in the decade when Catholic mothers named their babies after JFK, and died in the first week of September 2021. He attended St. Ann School, in Hornell, New York, and graduated from Hornell High School. His short marriage produced a beloved daughter, Andrea Koehler Easterbrook. Except for two brief ventures as a young man, attending Corning Community College and soldiering in Germany, he found no compelling reason to leave Hornell. Many of his poems describe imagined visits to other towns, complete with the day's weather and supper with a family. As it was for William Cowper, John's employment history would be a succession of withdrawals from society. John was ultimately able to live in his own apartments by committing daily acts of unspeakable bravery. John was an American original. I doubt I will never know anyone else like him. He was bluntly honest to the point where he was liable to say anything in his soft voice; also naturally funny in person, at times almost boyishly playful, and on the page he can be bizarrely comedic at times. For the last poem he would ever write, the strikingly beautiful "The Laurels of the River," his hand-scrawled word *reindeer* was so unexpectedly funny it was a puzzler for me to decipher. If his titles can be inscrutable, they are more often a joy to sound out loud. Try reading the table of contents to this book without frequent grinning. His poetry burns with the naïve sincerity of an Edward Hicks painting; it has no reading tradition or regard for prosody. He sought to see manifestations of God in the quotidian world and in himself. My working title for John's collection was *Of God*, and it remains a good one, if not best. The poet is buried in St. Mary's Cemetery, Fremont, near Hornell.

While I am confident that John didn't read *The Circus of the Sun*, or go to school on any contemporary poet, it is equally evident that the poems of John Koehler and Robert Lax have much in common, especially what I would call their "of God" affinities. I mean that John developed his poetry unaware of the creative spirits, including Lax, Adelaide Crapsey, and Sanford Plummer, of the area which chose him more than he chose it. If Lax's work had no influence on John, our knowing something about Lax can help us to read John's poems. Lax could be mistaken for Koehler when he wrote, in his journal:

I want to write a book of praise, but not use the religious words. That is because they should not be used lightly, and all the words I will be using must be used lightly, set down tentatively. The holy words hold terror for some, are not respected by others. I will try to talk in little words that people respect and do not fear. They respect them like hammers, they fear them no more than they fear doors or windows.

(Lax journal, 30 October 1944, Columbia University)

Robert Lax, poet and eremite, was born and died in Olean, New York. He lived in many places, from Manhattan to Paris and Patmos, but always returned to Olean for extended periods. John's maternal grandmother had been born in Olean when Lax was in grade school there. Lax is perhaps most remembered today for his friendship with Thomas Merton. The poets shared a cabin in the woods around Olean, on the eve of the Second World War; many critics believe their rustic lifestyle and literary preoccupations herald the Beats. He began writing his masterpiece, *The Circus of the Sun,* squirreled away in the St. Bonaventure library. Lax happened to be convalescing in Olean the month Donald, Connie, son Stephen and baby Kathleen took up residence in the village of Hornell, about fifty miles east of the college that son would one day attend. It was during baby John's first year that Lax was using Olean as his base for travel in the country. Lax was teaching the fall semester at Alfred State when John started second grade in nearby Hornell; when John was a twenty-three-year-old soldier stationed in Germany, Lax was visiting professor at St. Bonaventure. At the time of Lax's death in Olean, in 2000, John had begun to write the poems in his first notebook. It's spooky to run across a journal fragment for which John seems to approximate Lax's signature thin vertical line. Lax and John were gentle souls, mild mannered, humorous, solitary, spiritual, quiet tending to shyness. Once, out of the blue, John asked me to define *laconic.* Perhaps the rarest aspect of their poetry, and a major strength, is almost complete abnegation of poetic ambition. Putting aside the question of the Jewish Lax's conversion to Catholicism, the major difference between them is the older poet's wanderlust. Lax seemed to be forever traveling, often living abroad, only to return to southern New York. As a fictional character, Lax would be Bulkington; John was more the Wakefield type. However, very much like Lax before him, John was a poet of learning to live in his own skin.

In the best poems, we have John thanking God for the beauty of creation and, in turn, the world of words. Rather than employ symbols in his poems, he used code words to stand for a private array of concepts. I believe this process is more prosody than pathology. For example, while the word *less* expresses loss, it also holds a mystery for John Francis not unlike Robert Lax's aesthetic-by-subtraction. And the word *chew* (and its phonetic variations *chow* and *choo*), *choo* making the sound of a ptarmus from the disdainful poet's mouth, turns out to be code for Chief Operating Officer. The word *less* is written in the lexicon of the gentle namesake Francis, while *chew* comes like his fiery namesake John the Baptist crying in the wilderness. John showed a St. Francis kindness to what he calls "my little friends" in "The Silver Rain," especially to toads and tiny snakes in his yard. (Lax named *Circus of the Sun* after the song by Francis, "Canticle of the Sun.") John the Baptist ate grasshoppers and wild honey. John could be playful about the John/Francis dichotomies in his life. The four-foot holy statue of St. Lucy that he kept in his apartment, her eyeballs displayed like grapes on a serving plate, must have also reminded him of his former life of world-class drinking exhibitions at Lucy's Bar.

The poetic record of John Koehler's agon with life is fresh, sometimes raw, in part because it is unfettered by the Confessional poets he never read. The poems are more devotional than confessional; they are, to use John's code, "Of God" and not the intellect: closer to Job than Lowell. "Of God," in poem titles and dialogue balloons, is strung through John's journals—starting on the cover of the first journal and spilling over onto the end cover—like beads on a rosary. The "of God" clusters were clearly reminders for John to meditate and invited him to fill in the blank prefix. For John was a spiritual seeker of God in the world. Often, "____ of God" worked like a prompt and resulted in a poem.

Some "Of God" text boxes bring to mind work by contemporary conceptual artists like Sean Landers and Kay Rosen. Here's a sample:

SUNNY RAINY PIGEON DAYS

*

acropolis

peony

of

God

*

potato

white SLIPPERS

of God

*

it's rainin
harder
than
a
Truck

*

PAUSE: is the title of this program.
less cold meat loaf…

*

¼ of my life

thinking

LIGHTS ON

NOT EVEN DARK OUT

YOU TOO??

*

soup's

a carriage

Check your

horse?!!!

When I drove up to Hornell, he'd have me read his newest poems (always after midnight to the accompaniment of acid rock) but he never asked for criticism, and I gave only support. I must have been reading from the notebooks collected posthumously in *The Bear Who Came to Town*. John took years to finally ask my advice on how best to organize a sequence of poems—this turned out to be his only publication, posts between 2004 and 2007 on the Poetry.com database. (Even then, he seems to have had misgivings: we have the uncorrected proof page, from March 1, 2005, for "The summer of cholera" that he never returned.) A sister's memory of young John at the dinner table writing in the air with his finger his invisible rebuttal to their father makes me think of his reluctance to publish his words as an adult. At the time I came to know him, the room he slept in was an extension of his notebooks. He wrote on everything. In his hypergraphia, he even repurposed an old college notebook, after pages of entries for a sociology class, as a repository for his poems. He was our Robert Walser.

John was working on a poem at the end, revising "The Laurels of the River" as if to get it right. He left the finished poem beside a cup of coffee with the Catholic channel on the TV. I hope someone who loved John thought to toss a pen into his coffin so he can write on everything in eternity.

Rich Blevins
November 2021/March 2022

THE BEAR WHO CAME TO TOWN

The Bear Who Came To Town

Coming home from school, gypsum,
still summerish—then a dark blur,
it ran after us into the downtown,
the police went the other way, no slur.
At the hardware store it sought lunch,
people who looked crazy hurried along,
we ran and stopped, stopped and ran,
in the air I could hear 3 door song.
We circled on back and tried to creep,
then it surprised us, it flipped us off,
it jumped high in the air, pivoted,
then it was a pretty girl who smiled
and coughed.

GLENS FALLS

The sunlight in autumn, sad to change,
a full slate of activities can't compare to
this. Later in the year I'll forget, but not
now. Somebody left a bike there once, this
beautiful place. Soon GOD will bring the
rains again, and this "apple tree" of a day
will vanish, into the unknown of bewildered
sadness, maybe for days and years left behind,
or perhaps how much I take for granted,
then it's all gone on this Saturday, the road
mildly hot under the sun. Think I'll keep
this day like an old hat, a best friend,
to remind me what's gone, but also the beauty I kept.

DYNAMICS IN A STREAMING 'BOSE

The dinner bells enabled six,
here we go again, oh, her coat too,
the evening bronze medal elsewhere,
old photographs on our carpet grew.
The new place we just won't miss,
in town without nary a star,
we've crushed them down quite enough,
at least it's less his steel guitar.
The motorcycle really really worked,
bought from a fence in Venice,
all of these years without a home,
should we go do that or straight tennis.

THE WAKEFIELD ANGEL {OF GOD}

Winter set in, the roofs all left angled,
a few lights flickered, like breath,
overhead the sky ominous, elves evil,
one came for life, the other for death.
In a remote corner of town came
out of the night an orange glow,
some people stirred, others slept,
by the trains a homeless man blinked,
and a puzzled security guard suddenly wept.
Seven silver pieces and then he came,
into the spot where he spat on a leaf,
he thought of a rosary and felt sudden pain,
the Angel, he won, and less "good grief."

To Tis Dis Whole World

Still obligated to hand signals,
it goes one-two, scary death water,
to absorb the blame of satan mother,
and the wrath of God, who taught her?
Sometimes along the way crying,
knowing it's another trip to death,
for this boy too is guilty of
baptism in unholy water, death.
Now it fights me on all fronts,
God may or may not notice,
it's all fair, not to me, the blame,
for my coming is GOD'S shame.

Sumpter(A)

Those birds in GOD'S sky are not brimming with genius. They went one way, and went three, now two-of one. Later on, down the road, the puzzle beginning to clear, merge, we fight off more spittle bombs, from those who have become devoid of sanity. The bees aren't their keeper, though God may clean their house. If you leave your coat in the middle of a storm, it won't be retrieved, but will you. I'm hoping to be with God forever, it's a good plan. It's free, peaceful, with much protection. Put the damn swords down.

Rhine Country Dream

As twilight approaches, couples scurry to and fro, a day ending and for others, beginning. As the last light hovers around the Sidewalk Cafe a bird soars north across the European sky. A young mother sits pensively in a corner. She could be brooding or happy or both and neither. She reaches down and caresses her child's arm and makes a silly face. She is thinking about an American couple she hopes are united and maybe thinking of her also. She feels God and wipes a tear off her cheek. She pinches herself. She has freedom. Life begins. Again.

NEW YORK CITY AT NIGHT

The earlier rain a cleansing,
the streets teeming, as colorful people
go to and fro, non-deserters in the night,
a magnificently lighted church steeple.
A woman with blue hair screaming happy,
about something I just can't know,
an older man and teen boy talking,
delicious smelling food, beginning of a show.
On a street less populated there go
a solitary man and a dog on the loose,
a police car stopped and a woman in drag.
This is my life it's the one I choose.

No Clay Today In My Corner

Overhearing a strange conversation,
mom explaining to older brother
that this is merely the way,
the grape nuts are for no other.
Heard who they spoke of to please,
the torturer, the gun, and burser,
bluegrass in my corner of maple st!
All those games in a dome called carrier.
Going to school the very next day,
I felt sad for my brother,
going through all these things,
all because somebody needed a smother.

GREY WOLVES ROAD

[at the Greytan is Rushford Lake]

From a standing position, looking inward,
feeling partly blue from the unknown,
everything may be beautiful in there,
or a horror too real to ever know.
The early morning ashy fog like smoke,
not a single car anywhere in sight,
some lights on in the house up the road,
strange to feel obligated to that stranger.
Though the sun is up, the smell is rain,
don't know if to turn around, or through it again,
thoughts pleasant to gloom flickering in and out,
so left it to God, to show me my life.

To Find Another Street Home {Of God}

A quietness, unusual, on a milder winter night,
snow flakes, a beautiful song left behind,
all the way through, then sway to the right,
I thought of a long lost snow angel.
The sky seemed hidden by ever gray,
only a few random fools, to all moms,
when God made winter, this was what.
Onward, locomotives that belong to "frommes."
Here is my street, not set on a hill,
houses with night lights, but not a sound
if horses flew, here they would be found,
up the stairs, heater noises, a beer to pound.

THE SILENT WINTER NIGHT

The silent winter night like a warning
of something forgotten, unfinished,
in a time of life long ago,
as a child seeing stars, none diminish.
Timeless flurries brushing the street light
as an ageless man happens by and
he does glance my way, sudden guilt,
streams of snow possessing the night.
Then I remembered, took out one quarter,
a shiny quarter and put it outside,
the man was gone suddenly out,
night turning back into beauty.

The Doctor Office

Pages turned, a few years
behind. The sun made
a bar on the wall.
Thirteen minutes stationed
here. Waiting for my
name when they call.
A salesman bustled through,
said he was way behind,
a man talked about a dog,
a woman she called me
in, while I waited for
the Doctor.

Spraying Trees

He is a football hero, but
mostly a daddy. In the
air that smelled of wheat
and sage—my daddy
sprayed and sprayed
and sprayed. Then I
told my daddy to add
an -s to prayed. Then
we drove home and it
was nice.

THE SUMMER OF CHOLERA

On a day somewhere else before I
had played these games—that comes later.
The "parents aglow"—I tossed him a football,
him about four, and less he just dates her.
There was a secret place to go and think,
where I'd oust troubles, the grass turn pink,
then alpha, omega, quite a brook down there,
less there'll be help from the yellow link.
As a grownup in life, starry eyed t.v.,
a man without his helmet, a legend to me,
and the wars wage on, now too a parent,
let those ones go up, back to my tree.

A Purple Summer

The night was quiet, water flickering,
the river seemed moody, crass.
An "element" of fear rising in the air,
the four towels and then just one.
Feeling enormous wave of relief
startle through me like lost time,
secrets that never betrayed me,
though I'm sometimes "doubting thomas" too.

LIGHTNING REACHES

The lights splayed upward and more,
the band was only crickets and friends,
a peace feeling hard to match, yet,
unequal doom or loss swam in too.
The cold lake rippled into itself,
someone down the road yelled,
the bluebird lady got it in-too,
So why does life feel so blue?

MYRNNA INN

The shades had been opened, properly,
to reveal the beautiful German countryside,
quite warm for spring, though business slow,
a car entered, a man waved, then left.
She was 62 and in good health,
he died young, though his presence strong,
over coffee and prayer, she just knew
that stranger, this perfect day, a sign.
Been struggling with self-worth, sorrow,
a young couple with infant, entered,
she felt the breeze hit her, it smelled
like Heaven, on only this day.

SABBLEAU COUNTY

He drove slowly, though traffic was sparse,
this was new territory, though familiar,
something felt wrong here, accelerates.
The barn up ahead, strange vibes.
There was huge statue of some kinda elf,
a pipe in mouth, blazing greenish yellow eyes,
there seemed to be 25₡ pieces all near his feet,
he felt cold, hot, and suddenly sick.
Thirty years later, his secret remains,
though not religious, he felt, feels evil,
that day, that road, the young man he was,
all now seems fraud, devoid of light,
somebody else's life, sure could
use a new St. Francis one.

THE TEACHER

She was pleasant, quite, good smile,
her class liked her a lot, but,
there was something, she looked away,
catching a steely look from a redhead.
So now her kids know too,
her boyfriend left her for this,
never understand how or why,
a child asked a pleasant question,
order was restored, temporarily.
The day ended, she put her head
down, and vowed to keep those
two numbers, the ones juveniles
can even retain, in her mind
and heart forever, or until the
next spin.

The Marsten House

The flowers bloomed, set back coldly,
strange music emanated from, nowhere,
a car down the street, through it daytime,
a secret horrible town, doom to bloom.
The bookshelf inside crammed with lies,
of children with faces, cast from dye,
of trim plants not failed, and men
who told lies, a doorbell that
rang creepily, with nobody outside.
It sits at the end of the road,
without servants, keepers, or pride,
looking up at the hill, I saw
a fiery ring, looked off and
away, and got on my bike again.

[UNTITLED]

From up in the attic, there
came a funny sound, like a
man without lungs, or rats
chewing on cords. I looked up
and saw Mary, and my day
belonged to me again.

WONDER

Sometimes I look
out on stars, and
wonder why everything
turned out the way
that it did.

THE BLUES SWEPT AWAY
THE SOUTH RIVER

She was my "roommate" in college and she was
night meeting day in the army. She left me a
bedstand and I gathered her irony. A Priest
with a paisley tie—if you look once, look twice
away, for GOD allows me to register it all.
The nights on the loans can be passive,
possession is neither "whirlies" nor trees.
Once as a child we went to the barber,
and I saw instead the "imperial sea." On the
morning side of the mountain "she" and I
once planted a tree she said "what's the
mess?" and I said "don't cry for me!"

THE THREE MINUTE MIRACLE

We shop at night, we always have,
pulling into the lot, watchguard light,
we're old though, miss very little,
their boy a father of medium height.
A boy ran up with a scruffy burlap friend,
while I held their beer bag,
the boy he knew just what to do,
"two months of hell and the tuesday rag."
The ill man got up, he held forth,
he held gratitude and smiled not blue,
he thanked us all quite profusely,
and said to angel, "I've got two younger
than you."

FOOTBALL GAME ALTERNATIVE

A guy not really into all this,
park in a new place, walk kinda fleshy,
might have those power lines figured,
less nolan ryan, or don henley takin a piss.
The breeze settled down, away power,
threw the energy bar, fat'll do,
she strolled along faster than day,
blue shirted president, less M. COO.
Getting on back to car number two,
seeing a hoody guy skulking away,
got behind the wheel my hair swimming,
in spite of my mischief, the wife is to stay.

At A Quarter To Seven

We finished with supper, washed the dishes to let them dry.
A fragrant song finished on the radio. We took daughter for a
walk. The snow was beautiful and the air was full of unseen
static. I almost slipped and we all laughed. A car drove by so
I pretended it was just a car. My daughter stopped laughing
and seemed quiet, uneasy. Happiness left as swiftly as it had
appeared and the winter set in.

Seven Days In A Week Growing

Having heard some living voice,
more disgusting than all sound ever,
there is better, biblical and heavenly,
amidst ultrasounds perfected without clever.
A seed that can grow in boyhood,
for those who wish to dream,
of a decent life, yes; too for girls,
mothers and fathers give help the same.
In a quiet house, the homework done,
the garbage out, long lives, lurking,
so much more than that evil voice,
prodding vile filth and "jerking."

HIDDEN LADDERS

Missing those days in May,
those songs, and driving along.
Feeling life's defeats in between,
fall here, things feel wrong.
The "lawn" even I miss,
her days gloomy and nights dark,
cold brook downstream, no moon,
no children playing in the park.
Heard a song to bring this back
goosebumps, crickets, a slow death,
puzzling memories of better hope
outback stillness, don't miss "beth."

COSMO DRIVE

At the age of three I
started to notice streets.
Where other people live
and there life is complete.
Some houses more flowers
than us, others trouble
with paint or rust.
As I thought of cosmo drive,
I thought of airplanes,
and my last day of being
alive—I ride my bike too.

THE SILVER RAIN

The streets were quiet and the air smelled of beauty. Never can I forget all those little Angels. Then with a twinkle of light they were gone. It made me sad at first, though my mind wondered how much God could show us if we asked. The thirty seconds or so of rain left and so did all of my little friends. Every time early December comes around I take a walk and let my mind drift upwards to where the most beautiful things in all of the world went back to once, on a dark night, when just for a moment my life felt truly perfect.

Cova De Iris

There were wings on my ceiling,
and black spiders on my back,
a hockey stick lady "of grace,"
who took the fifth grade out of "crack."
One day I flew, my mind into snow,
although now I'm just thirty-two,
my toting sponsor all too clean,
one more bullet, sweet lady, then I'll truly
be "chew."
In a dream, on a faraway fence,
scary dogs caught uninstalling saints,
time has crept upon, to throw away my life,
like laundromat pence.

The Battle Of Waste

The grayish looking bull, spots still,
on somebody else's sink.
A faint tickle of a November breeze,
falling and falling, death on a tree.
Over yonder people shift with things
in their yard-evening supper looms,
as I thought of chewed baseball cards,
the last one I saw was "pat coombs."
Later on in life, in a church turned gray,
my ears stunned by even, priests,
the alarm clock chiming-ago summer moms,
and newspaper misspellings, above the crease.

CLOUDS OVER THE MONKEY BARS {OF GOD}

The church bells startled some,
on this grayish, self contained, day in Lent.
Overhead the hills seemed to wake,
JESUS seems to die again, so we live.
A family got in their car, they went,
light music left with them,
and morning began at 3 o'clock,
on an afternoon called Good Friday.
We walked by the stream, solemn,
the sun finally broke through,
made the day seem like another year,
through the static, birds knew what to do.

DUST SETTLES THE SNOW O' ST. DAMASUS

In the space between winter there,
springs hope of white light to renew,
people channeling their very lives,
some go it alone-others a family crew.
If Jesus came into the town,
on this warmish late February day,
my feeling is He'd find much here is
good, and the children, He'd watch them play.
On a different side of the world,
where tentative peace has stalled war,
a bird glides lithely into the sunset,
drops of rain parting the world's inner door.

ALMOST SUMPTURE

The fittings on the rings erode,
televisual fantia almost to pass,
in every custom there is writ closure,
to those who disroot our happiness.
That which is the possessor of the "wrong,"
on film like your heart on yellow,
the "TANK" saint welcomes the convert,
never the donkey of drudgery or delusion.
The valley's hills draw together,
the "morlockian" burlesque dance card done,
GOD'S children young and elder, too remain.

CASPITIVITY

In the summer of love, there came a rat,
saved, she was, by a man in blue,
who bore a cross with a KING and goo,
then he became a baby, of big bertha zoo.
For three sprite days, they killed me off,
strange evil beings without a thought,
then the rat was gone, a hellish blip,
and in steve's room, in a crib I later caught.
Thirty some years later, the hatred stays,
and that baby....well, he doesn't date my mom,
and the evening beer, old bullet in my back,
please use the toothpaste, or they might make
it crack.

GOD IS DRIVING

He drove home, feeling interior change,
he enjoyed his work, his life good.
He keeps picturing his father, a war hero.
This job will just not do anymore!
He saw fire alight in the sky, the
dignity and pride of the soldier,
who may never come home. There will be time
to teach again later, when we finish up this
war, there would, will be, well to believe.
Several months of safety, have gotten rather
good at this, then heavy footing, like a cloud
if it could call, never saw the bullets, never
felt his fear. He didn't go to die. He went to
finally live, like so many before him.
She never forgets her teacher, like a
brother-dad, and friend. She goes to the tree
to pray quietly to GOD THAT later she can
tell him he's a Friend.

GROUND ZERO

The son down, the day dark forever,
like something stolen, a cruel dream,
then they were there, weary with me,
at least a hundred ANGELS all and MARY.
Out of the night came a bird, of sorts.
A demon or devil, perhaps armageddon,
with a look away, and a quick look down,
it burst into flames and time stood still.
Tried to process what I'd seen,
in that Pennsylvania town, so much like home—
with an evil gown, then the sun came back up,
and the world waited.

In Independence Of Thee {Of God}

With HER parents shining and true,
to absorb this only a "syracuse" angel,
this wonderful little child looked at me,
and let me tell HER about her life.
In the distance the wind blew,
somehow noticed SHE of HIS tears,
SHE knew it all, SHE told me,
though SHE said nothing, I felt all of my years.
THEY were kind and gracious,
feeling so in awe and a little less in shame,
when SHE smiled and said "that to me,"
my heart trembled, and I said out loud HIS name.

Living Sppirit Of God

The big tree grew true,
unaided by rains, then yellow,
like a rush of wind She stood,
rather have the toad than that fellow.
From many miles away, a sly knive,
brought to me through my sinning,
and saved by the Sinless, less self,
and vans that aren't always grinning.
On the mean streets, and country too,
life brings problems without answers,
for we ding to the wrong experts,
when our CREATOR can kill, all of life's cancers.

Rain Falls In Austria

I took a book that I'd found,
a book from long ago, fragrant,
that used to fill me with help,
against the cold world-with tremors.
Against my own life swimming,
in a sea that rotted to malachy,
in a room with two mirrors,
without hooks or a dispensary of time.
On a day without the car agile,
and the wind seemed to spit in my face,
on the revolving recycled base of life,
I found some love and hope to chase.

Snow Fire 2/3 {Of God}

Once there was a rippling fire,
with days gone to remember,
pondering a future with curtains,
till there "lie" only smoldering ember.
Never expecting to find answers,
yet staring icily all the same,
finding only orange puzzlement,
and the leering flicker of flame.
It produced outer warmth,
and filled the room with light,
yet the coldness that invaded,
on that eve of CHRISTmas, night.

T. Dodd Stripes

Even yesterday there was chow,
that didn't make me think of hate,
there were non severe customs,
that intermingled, at least less "kate."
When I left for a beer or two,
and to mail my family a letter,
a beggar kinda man walked on through,
yet he wasn't a horse, or extra vetter.
When I got to the place where lonelies
sometimes sing, a kitty sharp woman
of at least nineteen told me a joke,
she said "who took away all the men?"

The Suicide Rosary

Here's something for you, here's this,
my chains are still rattling from ago,
green flowers and holy baldies, play,
if you see "geggy" stop and say hello.
On a tall street with small houses,
where all the pretend Christians go,
here I come with fire and no air,
be in rome and make "her" a little ho.
On the evening side of your feet,
where black reindeers stalk to kill,
kindly pull down your pants,
and I'll make "you" a father of a little
girl.

THE COLOR OF TOAST

As isolated, to be that single leaf,
growing through even storms, hope,
the day turns itself thru each chasm
like petals that fell, still we cope.
In a place to the west they sing,
where brooding is left behind,
those times and places can be worse,
so each day can be a treasure to find.
The water looms peacefully, think,
of those childhood dreams, slanting trees,
maybe if my shoes were different colors,
I would not feel the breeze.

The Flower Vase

The day was cool, slanting towards fall.
Children were playing in the street with
detached interest. The mystery of summer
seemed to gleam and vanish. "Drug" kept guard
in his area. A popped basketball brought me
a deep gloom that I couldn't quite
understand. A cold beer in another place was
drunk by a teacher who would soon be in a
classroom. As I tried to sweep my mind clean
of poison nostalgia—a broken fence came back.
I thought of pine cones and hope and of LOVE.
Then I wondered what ST. Bernadette would do
in my shoes.

The Green Maggot Miracle

A newly proclaimed "saint," with,
murder in her eyes at a 1993 birth,
the fix still executing the telephone,
me, used subs, tylenol, and extra girth.
All this business will be stopped,
the fences are growing much too large,
as it dings inside to kill from within,
even have to put up with more "barge."
On a Sunday morning, restless, needing,
to be with GOD in my hometown church,
b. mahoney and crew give me "no quarter,"
is that the "restraining order,"
or just "dunking" lurch [todd].

The War Is A Pew Unfinished {Of God}

Back then God sent down lightning,
though the devil was smarter too,
than to wage a war with JESUS,
unwanted by most, on HIS home court, they flew.
On the sand and debris of foreign land,
our youth fight to not die, if they kill,
can they come home and see GOD again,
do their enemies' mothers cry too, phil?
On the quietest morning ever begun,
in a church now torn apart with fire,
I grabbed my shoes to run, undivided,
to the real MOTHER MARY, HER beauty to
desire.

THE WAY OUR LIGHTS BEGIN

Somewhere caught in the middle,
of a non-descript ashy day,
I stopped at a mall, unfamiliar town,
she was there, like mist, walking away.
My heart almost chimed, all walls within,
every ounce of my life I'd give her,
though I know not even her name,
how I passed through the door, not even sure.
Years later on a sultry quiet night,
with the news off and church tomorrow,
somehow in a way I can't quite know,
I love her even more, when she sleeps I feel sorrow.

Weapons Of "Mass" Destruction

They play all those games on Saturday,
a light for day, Church glowing in Christ,
the moon is for night, walking, work,
an effort made possible from above.
This may be the time to consider,
the things in our world amiss,
elementary and primary dysfunction,
war raging on, still no weapons found.
That church there is a gift from God,
though adam & eve couldn't know,
that evolution & revolution,
don't bring—love, sunshine, and winter snow.

Wind Blown Fool

Lying here in darkness, five,
hoping to die when they're through,
the fire stays in yellow curtains,
to get her out, I may kick back too.
Heavy rain, all glad I'm gone,
this time for good, not just four days long,
inside of the ceiling tile drowning,
back again to that place with creepy song.
The day grows short, summer taught,
on an endless ray, plundering down,
even good memories destroyed as there caught.
This loving family moving strong.

GREYHOUND SUNSHINE

The sunlight spilled a little on the floor.
Going home for the Holidays.
As for the others on the bus—
I felt a fleeting sense of unity.
The bus stopped in a small town.
Nobody got on the bus and it made me feel sad—
and Christmas in a busy house—
nobody cussing and it made me feel glad.
As we caromed down the road
Christmas trees were for sale.
I thought of hope, unity
and the birth of Christ.

[A Blessing]

Sometimes the road under our feet
is rocky—other times the road
is light and friendly.
But the one constant is The Lord
and His Mother are always here
for us. On this sunny day today
we ask for The Lord's Blessing
of the food we eat. Amen.

[Untitled]

Once there was a shadow,
a place to hang my coat,
songs were only simple music
thought I'd someday vote.

Then came the big storm,
slapped away my strident youth,
run—jump—don't smile now.
Years later—where's my street.

The Laurels Of The River

At the Y intersection of the river, the farther side flows all clear, milk and coffee nearest to me ashore, melancholy day—more here than reindeer. A drowning boy searching for a Rosary, his tale lost to a previous dying day, sun slanting upside down the hosiery. Staring at the silt—still looking for a way to move my life from shore to clearer water. That same Rosary in my pocket—I love my daughter.

A NOTE ON THE TEXT

For this book, I have made my selection from the three extant notebooks and individual poems scattered through the Koehler homestead and his apartment, fully aware that John must have written many poems he was too careless to preserve. John, like Lax, always looked to simplify his life—at one point, he threw his computer into the Canisteo River to be rid of it.

The black 80-sheet Mead notebook was in use at least from November 2001 to January 2002. Its entries are limited to scattered fragments and spare parts until the reward of the fully developed prose poem "Sumpter(a)" at the end. When we persevere, we can discern John working out what will become his themes and codes for the poems of the next notebook. If the poet seems sometimes to have a mouthful of pebbles, he just may be Demosthenes practicing. Here, we must be content to have "less" and "of God" introduced but not developed. Through one sister's diligence, an extra poem belonging to the black notebook was unearthed in its Maple Street drawer. Its August 24, 1998 date above John's initials would make the prose poem "Rhine Country Dream" the earliest extant item from this notebook, in this case used as a fair copy book. There is no evidence to link the prose poem with John's military service in Germany (1988-1989), however tempting.

The red 150-sheet Mead spiral notebook from August 2002 to January 2004 features what must be fair copies of the longer poems "lightening reaches," "Myrnna Inn," "Sabbleau County," "The Teacher," "the marsten house" (named after the evil house in Stephen King's *Salem's Lot*), and "the blues swept away the south river." "Grey wolves road" is one of two poems that turned up in his mother's room; dated August 2, 1998, it is the earliest poem we have from the red notebook. Rushford Lake, north of Olean, is *pleasant* on the surface—along with Oil Springs ("discovered" by a Franciscan missionary), among John's favorite spots—but *gloom[y]* on the bottom: engineers submerged two towns for the reservoir. The poet is looking into the lake, and himself—"From a standing position, / looking inward…." John's poems to nature, for all their buoyancy, can turn into fishing into the ruins. The other poem, "To find another street home {of God}," is the last poem we know from the red notebook. It was John's nature to come out for the little guy and against the establishment. Here, the owners of the locomotives (which were once the basis for the railroad town's boom economy) are *frommes*, failures like the "few random fools" he passes in the street. The rapid series of puns on "iron horses" and the industry which has flown, then the noises from the space heater at home end the poem with the writer internalizing the history of the place.

The blue 120-sheet Herlitz spiral notebook was repurposed some years after he took dutiful notes in it for a college Sociology class. Entries end in November 2005. These poems show a poet increasingly aware of his craft. The title poem and "Glens Falls" are confidently delivered in thirteen lines, as if streamlining the sonnet form. I took my cue from the packet John asked someone to type for <u>Poetry.com</u> and centered the poems from this notebook—I liked the dense blocks they make, like the wine stain that spreads through pages in another notebook, wishing I could preserve that form— and I was surprised to find the lines ended perfectly when I did. John's story-telling in "The bear who came to town" is superb—we come to realize the bear was an unapproachable "pretty girl" only when she "smiled / and coughed," and the poet brings us down to earth. In "At a quarter to Seven," the family unit he'd heard about in Soc class ("socialization > FAMILY IS VERY INFLUENTIAL," he'd duly recorded in this same notebook) is destabilized in a paranoid second: "A car drove / by so I pretended / it was just / a car." The poet's familiarity with a place in "Glens Falls" is neatly established by remembering "Somebody left a bike there once." And nobody but John would dare describe the alpha male power pitcher Nolan Ryan's walking "kinda fleshy" and throwing a power bar for a fastball.

Also tracked down at Maple Street are "Hidden ladders" and "COSMO DRIVE," two poems belonging to an unidentified legal-sized notebook sheet of paper dated September 2005 and also saved together on 5x8-inch notebook paper. John used only the last two pages of a small hardcover notebook, its compact size and shape dictating the shape of the poems, for writing "The doctor office" and "SPRAYING TREES."

None of the three poems left in his last apartment is written on a full sheet of paper. We have "Greyhound Sunshine," a version of his gift to his mother, on a page torn from a 4x6-inch pocket notebook. "Sometimes the road under our feet..." comprises a third of a sheet torn from another notebook. (It is initialed "JK," in the fashion of the blue notebook.) The yellowed paper shows pin holes, indications that John displayed the poem. "Once there was a shadow," which John ends with the speaker's haunted question "—where's my street[?]," was composed on the back of his tenant's housing contract for January 1, 2019.

John left four drafts of "The Laurels of the River," his last poem. The versions make it clear that he was having trouble deciding between "his tale lost to a previous day" and "his tale lost till another day." But to put the rhyme word *reindeer* into his poem, in all four versions, came naturally to mind, brightening its darker use earlier in "The Suicide Rosary." The manuscripts were rescued from the apartment by Chris and Kathy. His tale was not lost.

It is problematic to talk about what audience John was writing for— God is a possibility, or posterity—so some of the poems are cryptic, others personal. I have made the editorial decision to let his poems breathe, and refrained from crushing his poems under the weight of scholarly notes. Still, knowing that *Geggy* was his three-year-old sister's imaginary friend does invite family to remember and also make "The Suicide Rosary" accessible for a general reader. I have made no attempt to regularize, much less "correct," punctuation, spelling, or syntax in this book, keeping in mind the story of the editors' disfigurements of Dickinson's poems from the fascicles. I selected all the publishable poems from the three extant notebooks, the sandwich bag of last poems, and materials gathered from the Koehler homestead, fully aware that John must have written many poems he was careless to preserve. I fancy that dwellers in a future century will uncover at 133 Maple Street a trove of lost manuscripts. May *The Bear Who Came to Town* be only the first installment to a future Complete Poems. Just when this collection seemed ready for publication, one of John's sisters shined a flashlight into the crack behind his old dresser—revealing a maroon spiral notebook containing "A PURPLE SUMMER," "New York city at night," "Broken glass on Pearl St.," "No clay today in my corner," and "The silent winter night," each an essential poem.

RB

Made in United States
North Haven, CT
07 June 2022

19942307R00050